This Certifies That

_____

who has been baptized, on confession of
faith, was received as a member of the

_____

Baptist Church

of _____

on Sunday _____ *19* ____

and the hand of fellowship given.

_____ *Pastor*

_____ *Church Clerk*

A New

BAPTIST CHURCH MANUAL

Revised

Let all things be done decently and in order.—1 Cor. 14:40

JUDSON PRESS®
VALLEY FORGE

The name JUDSON PRESS is registered as a trademark in the U.S. Patent Office.

PRINTED IN THE U.S.A.

CONTENTS

SPECIAL NOTICE

In the matter of the organization of a church, in its corporate capacity as a holder of property, and in the matter of the election of trustees, pastors and churches should carefully advise themselves concerning the requirements of the laws of their state and should see that the demands of the law are exactly met. It is impossible to detail the requirements of the laws of the individual states within the limits of this Manual.

EXPLANATORY

The Baptist churches of the United States do not form a church, with enforced standards of doctrine or prescribed order of government, from which no congregation may vary. The total body of Baptists is designated as the Baptist denomination and not the Baptist Church because each separate congregation is held to be a church in itself, as were the local churches of the New Testament era. The millions of Christians who are members of these local churches determine for themselves the direction of their internal affairs. They do share together in associations and conventions at the regional, state, and national levels, where they seek each other's counsel about the scriptural application of their common principles and the best methods of church work and plan for missions and the establishment and support of educational interests and other matters. Their essential unity is found in the Bible and the common faith and practice which they severally gather from its teachings.

It is evident, therefore, that Baptists can have no formulated or authoritative creed to which all

Baptists must subscribe. However, there are certain generally held views by which Baptists have identified themselves. Of course, Baptists hold many of the great cardinal doctrines of Christianity in common with other evangelical bodies, but there are distinguishing differences. This Manual explains some of those differences and sets forth the principles and practices of the Baptist denomination. It is intended also to serve as a short handbook for church officers and workers. Originally prepared by Dr. J. Newton Brown, and first published in 1853, it has gone through many editions and been circulated in many thousands of copies among Baptists the world over.

CHURCH COVENANT

One of the ways in which members of a local church express their common commitment is through a Church Covenant which describes their relationship to God and to one another. Many local congregations have developed their own covenants out of their experience. Over the years, many other congregations have used a covenant like this to express their mutual faith.

Having been led, as we believe, by the Spirit of God to receive the Lord Jesus Christ as our Savior, and on the profession of our faith, having been baptized in the name of the Father and of the Son and of the Holy Ghost, we do now in the presence of God, angels, and this assembly, most solemnly and joyfully enter into covenant with one another, as one body in Christ.

We engage, therefore, by the aid of the Holy Spirit, to walk together in Christian love; to strive for the advancement of this church in knowledge, holiness, and comfort; to promote its prosperity and spirituality; to sustain its worship, ordinances, discipline, and doctrines; to contribute cheerfully and regularly to the support of the ministry, the expenses of the church, the relief of the poor, and the spread of the gospel through all nations.

We also engage to maintain family and secret devotion; to educate our children religiously; to seek the salvation of our kindred and acquaintances; to walk circumspectly in the world; to be just in our dealings, faithful in our engagements, and exemplary in our deportment; to avoid all tattling, backbiting, and excessive anger; to abstain from the sale and use of intoxicating drink as a beverage; and to be zealous in our efforts to advance the kingdom of our Savior.

We further engage to watch over one another in brotherly love; to remember each other in prayer; to aid each other in sickness and distress; to cultivate Christian sympathy in feeling and courtesy in speech; to be slow to take offense, but always ready for reconciliation and mindful of the rules of our Savior to secure it without delay.

We moreover engage that, when we remove from

this place, we will as soon as possible unite with some other church where we can carry out the spirit of this covenant and the principles of God's Word.

DECLARATION OF FAITH

Baptists believe that each person has the right and responsibility to read and interpret the Bible, relating its message to his or her experience. At the same time, Baptists have developed expressions of their faith in ordered form for the sake of communicating that faith to others. Many "Confessions of Faith" have been developed for this purpose. One such Confession of Faith which has been meaningful for many Baptists is the New Hampshire Declaration of Faith which was adopted by the Baptist Convention of New Hampshire in 1833. The following statements summarize that Declaration of Faith.

1. The Old and New Testament Scriptures were written by men divinely inspired and are the only sufficient and perfect rule of faith and practice (2 Tim. 3:16; 2 Peter 1:21; Matt. 24:35; John 5:39).

2. There is one God, and only one, who is self-existent, eternal and infinite in every excellence, and who has revealed himself as Father, Son, and Holy Spirit, the same in essence, though distinct in

personality (Isa. 45:21; Deut. 6:4; John 1:1-14; Rev. 1:8; John 14:26; 15:26; Matt. 28:19).

3. Man and woman were created innocent but by voluntary disobedience fell from that holy state; so all humankind are now sinners, not by constraint but choice, inclined to evil; and therefore under just condemnation to eternal ruin (Gen. 1:27, 31; 3:1-6; Isa. 53:6; Rom. 1:18; 3:23).

4. Jesus Christ, the Son of God and the Son of man, came into the world to save persons from the guilt and condemnation of sin, offering his blood as an atonement and making that atonement available to all who exercise faith in him (John 1:29; Acts 4:12; Rom. 3:21-26; John 3:14-16; Matt. 26:28).

5. The result of acceptance of Jesus Christ is justification, whereby we are brought into a state of peace and favor with God (Eph. 1:7; Rom. 5:1).

6. The means whereby justification is secured are repentance and faith, through which we turn to God in sincere contrition and accept Jesus Christ as an all-sufficient Savior (Acts 2:38; Eph. 2:8).

7. God has his purposes of grace in the salvation of persons. These purposes are made effectual by the

giving of his Son and in the constraining and regenerating influence of the Holy Spirit upon all who sincerely believe in Christ. But these purposes do not contravene the freedom of human will nor render inoperative the proclamation of the gospel to all (Eph. 1:4; John 6:44; 1:12-13; 16:7-11; Eph. 2:10; Phil. 2:12-13; Rom. 10:13-16).

8. Nothing can separate true believers from the love of God; but they are kept by the power of God, through faith and salvation, the sure proof of this being their patient continuance and progress in righteousness and true holiness (Rom. 8:35-39; John 10:27-29; 2 Peter 1:3-4; Matt. 24:13).

9. The ordinances of the gospel are Baptism and the Lord's Supper. Baptism is the immersion in water of a believer in Christ, "in the name of the Father and of the Son and of the Holy Spirit," and symbolizes the fact of regeneration. The Lord's Supper is a commemoration of the dying love of Jesus and symbolizes the fact that the believer is continuously fed and nourished by Christ. In its observance, the Supper is to be placed after Baptism, according to its symbolic and historic

order and as required by the teaching of the New Testament (Matt. 3:6, 13-17; 28:19-20; Acts 8:36-38; Rom. 6:4; Col. 2:12; Matt. 26:26-30; Acts 2:41-42; 1 Cor. 11:23-29).

10. The church of Jesus Christ includes the whole company of believers of whatever name, age, or country, and is known only to the eye of God. The church which is visible to human eyes is a company of believers baptized in the name of the triune God and observing the forms, ordinances, and principles laid down in the New Testament (Col. 1:18; Eph. 1:22-23; 2:19-21; 1 Cor. 12:27-28; 1:2).

11. The first day of the week is to be observed as the Lord's Day or Christian Sabbath (John 20:19; Acts 20:7; 1 Cor. 16:1-2).

12. Civil government has been instituted by God for the sake of the common interest and good order of society; and government officials are to be prayed for, conscientiously honored, and obeyed, except only in those things which are opposed to the will of Christ who is Lord of the conscience and Prince of the kings of the earth (Rom. 13:1-7; Matt. 22:21; Acts 5:29).

13. Jesus Christ is to come again, judge the nations, and fill the earth with his glory and power (Matt. 25:25-51; John 14:3; Acts 1:11; 1 Thess. 4:16-17; 2 Thess. 2:3-8; Rev. 1:7).

14. There will be a resurrection of the just and the unjust—the just for blessedness and reward, the unjust for judgment and eternal doom (John 5:28-29; Matt. 25:31-46; Acts 24:15; 1 Cor. 15:22-24, 42-58; 2 Cor. 5:10; Rev. 20:11-15).

QUESTIONS TO APPLICANTS FOR CHURCH MEMBERSHIP

1. Have you prayerfully and thoughtfully considered the question of uniting with this church?

2. Can you say that you believe that you have met with a change of heart and that your sins have been taken away; that you love and trust Christ and will seek to follow all his ways; and that you enjoy prayer, the reading of the Word, the worship in the sanctuary, and the fellowship of Christians?

3. Have you carefully considered the doctrines of this church, and do you accept them as consistent with the teaching of God's Word?

4. Do you cheerfully accept the obligations imposed by the Church Covenant?

5. Do you promise to strive at all times to live peaceably with all others in the church, to be faithful to your duties, and to bear your share of the burdens and responsibilities that belong to the members of this church?

BRIEF HISTORY OF THE BAPTISTS

(For more complete information, see Robert G. Torbet, *A History of the Baptists,* third edition, Judson Press. Parts of the following summary are taken from the booklet *The Baptists* by John E. Skoglund, Judson Press.)

There are about thirty million people around the world who call themselves Baptists. They are divided into many different national and denominational groups. What is the common heritage which they share as Baptists? The answer to this question is more difficult than that for many other denominations. The Greek Orthodox Church, for example, traces its ancestry back to the days of the apostles. The Roman Catholic Church also claims its rootage in the earliest Christian centuries. The Lutherans trace their origins to Martin Luther, the Methodists to John Wesley, and the Disciples of Christ to Alexander Campbell and Barton Stone. But what about the Baptists? Where do they come from?

Many theories have been offered. Some say that Baptists stem from the movement of John the

Baptist. While the name "Baptist" and the practice of baptism upon repentance and faith are reminders of John's ministry at the Jordan River, Baptists have drawn upon other sources as well. The congregational organization of Baptists, with its stress upon the laity, is very much like the organizational pattern of the Jewish synagogue. It would be virtually impossible, however, to demonstrate a direct line between the Baptists and early Jews. There are others who have attempted to prove a direct continuity with the churches of the New Testament period. While certainly Baptists draw their faith and practice from the New Testament, the tracing of such historical continuity depends upon very sparse historical evidence.

In reality, Baptist history has many roots and branches. The real connection between modern Baptists and earlier Christians is not so much a direct historical link as a spiritual relationship. For instance, some modern Baptists identify themselves with ancients like the Montanists, who stood for the purity and spirituality of the church in a time of increasing authoritarianism and inclusiveness.

Other Baptists would find their spiritual ancestry in such medieval fighters for freedom as Peter Waldo, John Wycliffe, and John Hus—all of these fought on scriptural principles to bring back into the life of the church such neglected qualities as purity, personal responsibility, and freedom of belief and worship.

Some very competent Baptist historians see a spiritual likeness of Baptists and the Anabaptists of the Reformation period, a group of "left-wingers" who carried the biblical and theological principles of the Reformation to their ultimate conclusion.

Most present-day Baptist historians find the taproot of their life in the English Puritan movement in the early seventeenth century.

The English Baptists

In 1602 John Smyth, brilliant young Cambridge graduate, publicly denounced the episcopacy of the established church as being unscriptural. Such preaching brought immediate reaction from the authorities who had Smyth removed from his lectureship. As a result he joined a small group of

Separatists in Gainsborough who called him as their pastor. In most respects this group was similar to what has been known more recently as a Congregational church. When persecution in England became severe, John Smyth's Gainsborough group, along with another Separatist congregation, moved to Holland, and in 1606 his group formed a church in Amsterdam.

John Smyth's devotion to the purity of the Word of God drove him to an ever deeper research into the life, the spirit, the organization, the worship, and the practice of the primitive church. Two convictions emerged from his study.

First, Smyth concluded that the early church was a gathered church composed of those who had knowingly repented of their sins, had found forgiveness, and had accepted Christ as Lord and Savior. He declared that the rightness of a church did not consist in its external order, handed down through a succession of bishops, but rather in its being gathered by the Spirit of God and bound together in a fellowship of faith.

In this first principle Smyth was not out of step

with the English Separatists, but his second conviction proved to be more revolutionary. In addition to his personal study of the Bible, he undoubtedly was influenced by the Dutch Mennonites. This group took its name from Menno Simons, one of the influential leaders of the Anabaptist groups in Europe. The Mennonites, as Anabaptists, taught that a person should be baptized after making a confession of faith. (The name "anabaptist" comes from "re-baptize," because at that time almost all persons were baptized as infants.) Smyth came to the conclusion that the church should consist only of those who had repented of their sins, confessed their faith in Christ, and been baptized. In 1609 Smyth and thirty-six other members of his Amsterdam congregation affirmed that their infant baptism had not been valid, that they must be baptized as believers, and that henceforth the church should be limited to believers.

These early Baptists poured the water over the person being baptized, but as they studied the meaning of the word in the Greek New Testament further, they concluded that the meaning of the Greek word *baptizo* is "to dip under, to immerse." Hence they came to a new understanding of the significance of baptism by immersion as a symbol of the burial, through union with Christ, of one's past life and the emergence of a new life in Christ. The meaning rather than the form of baptism is primary. For Baptists, the local church is a gathered company of persons baptized upon profession of their faith.

A part of the Amsterdam congregation returned to England under the leadership of Thomas Helwys in 1611 or 1612. Helwys and his group settled in London. Each Sunday he led his little church in worship. He sent a copy of his book on liberty of worship to the king. This book declared that "men should choose their religion themselves seeing they only must stand themselves before the judgment seat of God to answer for themselves." King James responded to this denial of the king's authority in religious matters with fury and locked Helwys in Newgate Prison. Nothing further is known of him. But his words were the first unqualified English statement of the right to be free to affirm one's own position in matters of faith.

Baptists in America

The first Baptist church in what is now the United States of America was probably the First Baptist of Providence, Rhode Island, founded by Roger Williams in 1639. (The historical records leave some doubt as to whether this church or the Baptist Church in Newport, Rhode Island, was actually the first to be founded.) Roger Williams had come from England where he had some associations with the Separatist movement and settled in the Massachusetts Bay Colony. However, because of his belief in the freedom of every person to worship according to conscience, he was forced to flee from Massachusetts. He purchased a large tract of land in what is now Rhode Island from the Indians and established a new colony in which the settlers agreed that there would be liberty of conscience for all. Williams and John Clarke, pastor of the Newport church, secured a new charter from the king in 1663, establishing this principle of civil and religious liberty which has become a vital part of the American tradition.

During the colonial period, Baptists spread throughout the colonies, their cause being aided by the evangelistic fervor of the Great Awakening. Wherever they went, they continued their struggle for religious liberty. In 1707 the Philadelphia Baptist Association was organized, following the pattern of such associations in England and Wales. The association was regarded as an advisory council to the local churches and an expression of the larger church through which the mind of Christ might be made known. The number of Baptists in Virginia, the Carolinas, and Georgia grew rapidly in the period immediately preceding the American Revolution. The first Negro Baptist church in America was founded between 1773 and 1775 at Silver Bluff, South Carolina. Although the church was founded by a white Baptist preacher, a Reverend Palmer, a black man by the name of George Lisle carried on the ministry there. One of those converted under Lisle's preaching was Andrew Bryan. After the war, Bryan, with others, established the first Negro Baptist church in the state of Georgia in 1788.

In 1813 Adoniram Judson, who had sailed to Burma as a missionary under Congregationalist sponsorship, declared his belief while on board ship that the only valid baptism was believer's baptism as practiced by the Baptists. He appealed to Baptists in America for support. His colleague, Luther Rice, who shared Judson's conviction about baptism, returned to the United States to enlist support for Judson. As a consequence of this challenge from the field, the General Missionary Convention of the Baptist Denomination in the United States for Foreign Missions was formed, the first national organization of Baptists. This organization was followed by the Baptist General Tract Society in 1824 and the American Baptist Home Mission Society in 1832. Thus, Baptists were inspired to organize in order to fulfill the Great Commission of Christ.

As the American nation became divided over the issue of slavery, many of the Protestant denominations felt the strain. In 1845 the Southern Baptist Convention was organized by Baptist churches in the South, and the Northern organization was renamed the American Baptist Missionary Union, later to become the American Baptist Foreign Mission Society. In 1907 the American Baptist Publication Society, formerly the Tract Society, and the Home and Foreign Mission Societies, including the Woman's Home and Foreign Societies, entered into closer cooperation in the Northern Baptist Convention, now known as the American Baptist Churches in the U.S.A. The Southern Baptist Convention developed its own agencies for foreign missions, home missions, and education and publication.

The missionary motive was equally strong in the development of denominational unity among the Baptists of African descent. Their first independent organization of churches was the Providence Missionary Baptist District Association of Ohio, founded in 1836. After the Civil War, the Negro churches grew quickly, from a membership of 150,000 in 1850 to nearly 500,000 by 1870. By 1870 there was a Negro Baptist Convention in every Southern state. A number of other organizations followed, and in 1895 most of these were consolidated in the National Baptist Convention of America. As time went on, a segment of this group formed the National Baptist Convention of the U.S.A., Inc., and still later the Progressive National Baptist Convention was organized.

The influx of immigrants from many European countries, the Far East, and Latin America in the late nineteenth and early twentieth centuries led to the formation of several Baptist groups ministering to these people in their own language.

Because of the Baptist belief in the right and responsibility of every believer to interpret the Bible, a great number of smaller groupings of Baptists have been formed over the years. Some of these groups were later absorbed into the major Baptist bodies, and others have remained independent.

Overall, Baptists have made a significant contribution to the American scene through their emphasis upon religious liberty, the congregational life of the local church. and fervor to carry on the mission of Christ through the church.

BAPTIST CHURCH GOVERNMENT

I. As to Principle:

A. In the administration of its government and the exercise of its authority, the local church is not legislative but executive. It may develop its own usages and forms in the transaction of its business, but it cannot make laws vitally affecting its organization or government. It can only execute those already made by the Great Lawgiver, as laid down in the New Testament. In other words, the church is not a human but a divine institution (Eph. 1:22; James 4:12).

B. The church is not to be controlled by one individual or set of individuals; all are to share alike in its government, all questions being decided by the majority. The church may appoint committees to do certain work and may confer functions on individuals; but the church must do this, and the church must ever hold these committees and individuals responsible to it (Matt. 23:8-12; Acts 1:24-26; 6:5; 13:1-3; 15:22).

C. The church should hold itself aloof from all

alliance with secular governments. In the protection of its property and its rights, it may appeal to the state like any other company of citizens, but it should never receive patronage or ask for state aid in the enforcement of its faith (Mark 12:17; John 18:36; Acts 4:19; 5:29).

D. There should be interdependence, cooperation, and fellowship among the churches. There should be exchange of counsel when needed and wise leadership in carrying on the great denominational and missionary enterprises. But there should not be any great ecclesiastical organization exercising authority over the individual church without representation and participation in the decision making by the local church (John 17:21; Acts 15:1-31; Romans 15:25-27; 1 Cor. 16:1-3; 2 Cor. 8:1-4).

II. As to Form:

A. In the organization of a church, Baptists recognize only two church officers named in the New Testament: Pastor (called also Bishop, Overseer, Elder, Presbyter) and Deacon (Phil. 1:1; 1 Tim. 3:1-8; 4:14; Acts 20:17-28). Other officers, such as clerk, treasurer, trustees, etc., may be chosen by the church to fulfill specific tasks.

B. Baptist churches, while independent in their government, are yet, for various reasons, grouped into associations, according to their convenience of location with reference to each other. These associations meet yearly—each church within their boundaries being represented by delegates—for the purpose of gathering the yearly statistics of the churches, for instituting measures for carrying on any work which they have in common, for the consideration of questions of interest to the churches and the denomination, and for the exchange of fraternal greetings. Besides these associations there are city, state, regional, and national organizations for carrying on denominational and missionary work which cannot be done by the associations.

ORDINANCES

I

BAPTISM

I. Our Point of View

Baptists hold that this question is to be determined wholly by an appeal to the Scriptures. They believe that the Bible is the sole authority in matters of faith and practice and that baptism, to have any significance, must be based solely upon that. Baptists hold that the Scriptures speak plainly on the question of baptism; that, since baptism is a command imposed alike on all believers, it must be set forth in plain and unequivocal language so that all may easily understand it; and that the obvious meaning of Scripture in regard to it must be taken. Baptists also hold that the spirit of true obedience requires an unreserved and unquestioned submission to the commands of our Lord; that this obedience never asks what is essential but what is commanded.

II. IS BAPTISM REQUIRED?

Baptism was insisted upon during the ministry of Christ and throughout the apostolic ministry and was made a permanent requirement. The Great Commission imposes baptism on all believers alike without distinction of time, place, or circumstances. The command to repent and believe is no more positive than the command to be baptized (Matt. 3:15; Luke 3:3; John 3:5, 22, 26; 4:1; Acts 2:38; 10:48; 22:16; Matt. 10:32-33; 28:19; Mark 16:16).

III. WHO MAY BE BAPTIZED?

From the above references it will be seen that our Lord in his Great Commission enjoins baptism on only those who believe. Also Peter, on the day of Pentecost, said to the inquiring multitude, "Repent, and be baptized." As a result, "they that gladly received his word" were baptized (Acts 2:41), thus showing that they had undergone a change of heart before baptism was administered. Thus also the Samaritans were baptized "when they believed" (Acts 8:12). It was when the Ethiopian could say that he believed in Christ "with all his heart" that he was baptized (Acts 8:37-38). Not until Paul had been filled with the Holy Ghost was he baptized (Acts 9:17-18). Not until Cornelius and his friends had "believed" and "received the Holy Ghost" were they baptized (Acts 10:44, 47-48). It was when Crispus and his house "believed on the Lord" that they were baptized (Acts 18:8). Paul tells us that only those who are prepared to bury the old life of sin and accept the new life of holiness are fit subjects for baptism (Rom. 6:3-6). Peter tells us that baptism is "the answer of a good conscience toward God"; that is, the baptism does not make a good conscience, nor precede it, but is the result or reply of a good conscience (1 Peter 3:21).

From all this it appears that faith and repentance must precede baptism. It is upon the above understanding of the teaching of the New Testament that Baptists repudiate the doctrines of baptismal regeneration and infant baptism.

IV. WHAT IS BAPTISM?

This is an important question, for the reason that baptism is not a principle or truth in itself, but is the expression of a truth. It is held by some Christians that there are three forms of baptism: sprinkling, pouring, and immersion, any one of which is valid. This, Baptists maintain, cannot be, because baptism as a symbolic act must be definite and unvarying in its form.

A. There are only four passages from which the symbolism of baptism may be established. As referred to in John 3:5, it is linked with the idea of a new birth and is intended to be descriptive of that fact, since it is in reply to the question of Nicodemus concerning the nature of the new birth. Birth is the emerging from one state of existence into another and is fitly symbolized only by immersion.

In Rom. 6:3-5 and Col. 2:12 it is declared that baptism is designed to set forth the fact of death to sin and resurrection to a new life of holiness. The only baptism that can represent a burial and resurrection is immersion, whereby the whole body is laid beneath the water and raised therefrom. In Gal. 3:27 baptism is said to denote "the putting on of Christ," the allusion being to the act of enveloping one's self as with a mantle. This symbolism can be expressed fully only by the act of immersion.

B. Still further evidence may be derived from the word itself. "Baptize" is a Greek word, having never been translated but simply transferred into our English versions of Scripture. All Greek lexicographers agree that the primary meaning of the word "baptize" *(baptizo)* is "to dip," "to plunge," "to immerse." If the New Testament writers had wished to express the idea of "sprinkling" or "pouring," there were words in the Greek with these primary meanings which they could have used, but these words are never used by them in connection with baptism.

C. Much circumstantial evidence may be derived from the New Testament. We are told that the people who came to John "were baptized of him *in* Jordan" (Matt. 3:5-6; Mark 1:5); that Christ when he was baptized "went up straightway *out* of the water" (Matt. 3:16; Mark 1:10); that Philip led the eunuch "down into the water" and "up out of the water." Again we are told that John baptized in Aenon near Salim "because there was much water there" (John 3:23).

In reference to Acts 2:41, the question is sometimes raised, "Was there water enough at Jerusalem to immerse the three thousand, and could they all be immersed in one day?" Jerusalem abounded in tanks and pools, affording the most ample means for the administration of the rite. There was no obstacle to the use of the public reservoirs. According to actual test, the rite can be administered by immersion with ease and due solemnity once a minute. Less than one minute each was required to baptize the two thousand two hundred and twenty-two baptized in the Telugu mission some years ago by Doctor Clough and his assistants. The case of the jailer baptized in the prison (Acts 16:33) is sometimes cited as one in which immersion was not practicable. It is not positively stated that he was baptized within the walls of the prison. But if he were, this would form no obstacle to immersion; for baths and reservoirs were common appurtenances of houses and public edifices among the Greeks and Romans.

Immersion was the only form of baptism practiced from the time of the apostles until the third century of the Christian era, and to this fact practically all scholars testify. For quotations see Latourette, *A History of Christianity,* pp. 193-195.

II

THE LORD'S SUPPER, OR COMMUNION

This ordinance is designated in the New Testament by three expressions: "Communion," the "Lord's Table," and the "Lord's Supper" (1 Cor. 10:16, 21; 11:20). Its designation, the "sacrament," has perhaps grown out of the belief that when the bread and wine have been consecrated, they become savingly efficacious to those who partake. Baptists maintain that Communion is restricted in its character rather than unrestricted, although, practically, there is no such thing among evangelical Christians as unrestricted Communion. All insist that certain conditions must be complied with before coming to the Lord's Table. The question as to what restriction should be put upon this ordinance must be settled, not by our preferences, but by an appeal to the Word of God.

I. IS THE ORDINANCE OF COMMUNION TO BE RESTRICTED?

A. The Lord's Supper grew out of the Passover feast and is a substitution for it (Matt. 26:17, 26-29). Christ is called "our passover" (1 Cor. 5:7; compare also John 19:14). Both the Supper and the Passover symbolize the same great fact, only the one is retrospective and the other prospective. The Supper, therefore, must partake of the character of the Passover; and this doubtless was Christ's design in attaching it to that feast. But the Passover feast, by direct command, was restricted to the household. Only in case the family was too small to consume the lamb at one sitting were others to be allowed a place at the table, and they had to be next-door neighbors and intimate acquaintances of the family. (See Exod. 12:3-4 and 45-46.) The observance of the Lord's Supper by individual churches, which are so many distinct households in Christ, is an exact fulfillment of this requirement. Christ substituted bread and wine for the lamb, but he did not abrogate this restriction.

B. When Christ instituted and first observed the Supper, it was not in the midst of a general assembly of Christians, but in the midst of his chosen and intimate disciples (Matt. 26:20). The next mention of the Supper is in Acts 2:46, where it is expressly represented as being observed in households, among those who had with each other the most intimate Christian acquaintance and fellowship; and the same may be reasonably inferred from the allusion in Acts 20:7-11. The apostle Paul's argument in 1 Cor. 10:16-21 and 11:18-34 is for restriction in the observance of the Lord's Supper.

II. WHAT ARE THE RESTRICTIONS IMPOSED?

Faith in Christ and a Christly life are the chief prerequisites (John 6:53-57; Acts 2:46-47; 1 Cor. 10:16-21; 11:20-29). Besides the Lord's Supper, the the only ordinance instituted by our Lord was that of baptism, and that baptism should always precede the observance of the Supper the Scriptures clearly reveal.

A. This appears from the historic relation existing between the two ordinances. Our Lord instituted baptism at the beginning of his ministry (John 3:23; 4:1); he instituted the Supper at its close (Matt. 26:26).

B. The symbolism of the two ordinances requires this order. Baptism symbolizes the new birth (John 3:5; Rom. 6:4; Titus 3:5; 1 Peter 3:21). Communion not only commemorates the death of our Lord, but also symbolizes our spiritual nourishment in him (John 6:41-58; 1 Cor. 10:16, 17; 11:28-30).

C. This order is enforced by positive command. In all the commands pertaining to these two ordinances, baptism is placed as the first duty to be performed after repentance and faith (Matt. 28:19-20; Acts 2:38; 22:16).

D. This order was scrupulously observed by the apostolic church as far as we have any record. Not until after the three thousand had been baptized is there any account of their "breaking bread" (Acts 2:41-47). In Acts 20:7, "the disciples came together to break bread."

To this relation of the ordinances all

denominations of Christians practically agree. Baptists, however, hold that immersion and immersion only is scriptural baptism, and for this reason they are more restrictive in respect to the Communion than other denominations.

CHURCH DISCIPLINE

Baptists have no "Book of Discipline," but in such matters they resort to the Word of God as their only rightful authority.

I. THE DUTY OF CHURCH DISCIPLINE

The New Testament enjoins upon the church the duty of exercising discipline over its members. This is enforced as a positive command. (See Matt. 18:15-17; Luke 17:3; Rom. 16:17; 1 Cor. 5:5, 7, 11, 13; 2 Thess. 3:6; 1 Tim. 5:20.) The apostle Paul commended the Corinthian church for its careful and zealous exercise of discipline over its disorderly members (2 Cor. 7:8-13). Our ascended Lord approved the church of Ephesus, because "it tried them which say they are apostles and are not." On the other hand, he threatened the church in Pergamos with judgment because it retained those who held to "the doctrine of Balaam," and to "the doctrine of the Nicolaitans." He likewise reproved the church in Thyatira because it suffered "that woman Jezebel, which calleth herself a prophetess, to teach and to seduce" his servants (Rev. 2:2, 14, 15, 16, 20). If, therefore, the church is to expect the approval of its divine Head, it must keep itself free from false teachers and evil persons.

II. THE AIM OF CHURCH DISCIPLINE

A. The chief aim of church discipline, as set forth in the New Testament, is to save the offender (Matt. 18:15-17; Gal. 6:1; Titus 3:10). Even when it is impossible to bring the offender to repentance, and exclusion becomes necessary, one's spiritual welfare should still be the end sought. Indeed, the very act of exclusion is designed to awaken offenders to a sense of their condition and to a realization of the fact that they are not of the church but of the world (1 Cor. 5:5).

B. A further aim is to save others in the church who may be tempted into sin or corrupted by the evil example of those already guilty (1 Tim. 5:20; Rev. 2:20). The moral tone of the entire membership may be lowered by the bad example of one member.

C. A church should exercise discipline when necessary, in order that it may vindicate its own character. The church is of God, who loves the right and condemns the wrong; it is "the body of Christ," and he is "head over all things to the church." When, therefore, a church ceases to cherish the right and condemn the wrong, to oppose that which is directly opposed to Christ, it belies its divine origin, and all reason for its separate existence is at an end. Wherever sin openly manifests itself in the church, it is to be rebuked, and all who willfully oppose themselves to the plain requirements of the Christian life must be thrust without, having no part with the disciples of Christ (2 Cor. 6:14-16).

III. LAWS OF CHURCH DISCIPLINE

The New Testament recognizes three principal causes for discipline: personal difficulties, heresy in doctrine, immorality in conduct.

A. The law pertaining to personal difficulties is to be found in Matt. 18:15-17. When proper explanations and apologies are met by a refusal to be reconciled, it then becomes the duty of the church to consider the matter. In a case where neither party is willing to make any effort at reconciliation and the matter becomes a reproach to the church, it becomes the duty of the church to consider the matter even though the first steps, as above indicated, have not been taken.

B. The law pertaining to heresy in doctrine: "A man that is a heretic, after the first and second admonition, reject" (Titus 3:10). Differences of opinion on many doctrines and differences of interpretation of many passages of Scripture are natural and admissible. But a "heretic," strictly speaking, is one who is radically deficient in faith, who denies and seeks to subvert the fundamental principles of the Christian religion. Moreover, such a person is, as the Greek word implies, "a faction maker." One may use false doctrines to create division and strife in the church. One may have a bitter, bad spirit coupled with these errors. Such a one is to be admonished. If the person is in error through ignorance, and seems to show a teachable spirit, that person is to be borne with and admonished, not only once, but twice. If, however, one is incorrigible and hopeless, one is to "be rejected," which means thrust outside the church.

C. The law pertaining to immorality of conduct. This law prescribes three methods of procedure according to the gravity of the offense.

1. Sudden faults: "Brethren, if a man be overtaken in a fault, ye which are spiritual, restore such a one in the spirit of meekness; considering thyself, lest thou also be tempted" (Gal. 6:1). This is a case evidently where one, under the pressure of sudden and great temptation, has been surprised and overtaken with sin. And the sin into which one is led is not some gross wickedness, but is a "fault," a misstep. Such a sin is just that which the most "spiritual" under like circumstances and like temptations might fall into. The manner of dealing with such a person is to seek and restore the person, to reach out a helping hand, to encourage the person to undertake once more the path of rectitude as, no doubt, in the heart of hearts one desires. This need not be a formal act on the part of the church, but fellow Christians should go to a person individually and, by their sympathy and entreaty, seek to reclaim the person. If one has "the root of the matter," one will hasten to confess to the church as a whole.

2. Confirmed habits of wrongdoing: "Now we command you, brethren, in the name of our Lord Jesus Christ, that ye withdraw yourselves from every brother that walketh disorderly" (2 Thess. 3:6). This has reference to one who is confirmed in disorderly ways, "who walks disorderly," who makes that a habit, a mode of life. The manner of dealing with cases of this kind is left entirely to the discretion of the church. It must withdraw itself from these disorderly persons, but the mode of procedure is left to be determined by each case. The course to be pursued in one case may not be the best in another. It may be well to commit the investigation of one case into the hands of a committee specifically appointed for that purpose, the church to take the results of its investigations. It may be well to submit the details of another case to the scrutiny of the entire church. The manner of taking evidence in one case may not be possible in another. With some it may be well to go through a long process of what is called "labor"; that is, visiting them through committees and individuals and seeking to reclaim them. With others, this

course may be impossible, or it may be wholly uncalled for, it being evident from the very start that it will be useless.

3. Gross immorality: the full text of the law pertaining to this is impossible here to quote. We can only refer to the passage which constitutes the whole of 1 Cor. 5. It will be found that gross immorality is to be treated with promptness and unflinching severity. The honor of the church and the good of the cause may require immediate expulsion and without any reference to the feelings of the offender—it being impossible usually for the church or the individual, under the circumstances, to distinguish between sorrow for the discovery of the sin and that for the sin itself. See also 2 Cor. 7:11.

CHURCH PROCEDURE

I. CONCERNING CHURCH OFFICERS

A. The pastor is called by vote of the church and continues in office as long as both parties are agreed. The pastor's special duties are preaching the gospel, administering the ordinances, exercising pastoral oversight, and taking general guidance and care of the religious interests of the church and people.

B. The deacons are elected, by vote of the church, for a definite or indefinite period. Their duties consist in caring for sick and needy members, assisting in the administration of the ordinances, and in every way aiding the pastor in his work.

C. For convenience and expediency, other officers are, from time to time, elected for the purpose of looking after the many other interests of the church.

II. RECEPTION OF MEMBERS

A. Persons applying for membership in the church should be presented on recommendation of the pastor and deacons or on the recommendation of a committee on membership which the church may appoint.

B. No one should be received into membership without the unanimous vote of the church; unless the church, after due inquiry, is satisfied that persons objecting have no just ground for their complaint and are unreasonable in their attitude.

C. Persons applying for membership by baptism must give evidence of conversion and assent to Baptist faith and practice.

D. Members of other Baptist churches may be received on their letters of dismission, provided those letters are of recent date. Otherwise, they may be required to relate their Christian experience or give satisfactory explanation of their delay in presenting their letters of dismission.

E. Persons coming from other denominations, and who have been scripturally baptized,[1] or persons who were once members of Baptist churches but have lost their connection by long absence or for other similar causes, may be received after the relation of their Christian experience.

[1] In some parts of the country, baptism is required.

F. Persons excluded from the church may be restored after making due confession to the church and giving satisfactory evidence of repentance for their faults.

G. The right hand of fellowship is given to new members at the Communion service. It is designed simply as an expression of the welcome and fellowship of the church.

III. Dismission of Members

A. Members should be dismissed with the same unanimity with which they are received.

B. A member may be dismissed to the fellowship of another Baptist church by letter of recommendation.

C. A member uniting with another denomination may be dismissed by the granting of a certificate of standing; or membership may end by the simple erasure of the name from the roll.

D. A member under discipline found guilty of the charges made is by vote excluded.

E. Anyone receiving a letter is still regarded as a member of the church granting it and is subject to the authority and discipline of that church until received into the fellowship of another church.

F. A member under discipline is expected to refrain from active participation in the rights and privileges of membership.

G. A member who is excluded is officially notified thereof by the church clerk.

IV. ABSENT MEMBERS

A. Members removing permanently to the vicinity of a sister Baptist church should, as soon as convenient, take Letters of Dismission to that church.

B. Members intending to be absent temporarily should take with them letters of introduction to the church where they may be residing.

C. Members removing to a locality where there is no church of like faith and order should communicate with their church at least once each year.

D. Members absent for a long period without communicating with the church may be excluded for neglect.

PARLIAMENTARY RULES

I. BUSINESS MEETINGS

A. No important business should be done without an attendance that would be considered representative; and no meeting for the transaction of business should take place without previous notice.

B. The order of business may be suspended at anytime by vote of the meeting, or by the moderator, no one objecting.

C. Every business meeting should be opened and closed with prayer.

II. MOTIONS

A. All business should be presented by a motion, made by one member and seconded by another.

B. A resolution and an ordinary motion, when requested, should be presented in writing.

C. A question is not to be discussed until it has been moved and seconded and then stated by the moderator.

D. A motion before the meeting must be

disposed of before any other questions can be introduced, except questions of privilege.

E. A motion lost should not be recorded.

III. SPEAKING

A. Anyone speaking on a question should rise in place and address the moderator.

B. If two rise and address the moderator at the same time, preference is given to the one farthest from the moderator.

C. Anyone using improper language, introducing improper subjects, or who may be otherwise out of order, may be called to order by the moderator, or any member, and must be seated or conform to the rules.

D. No one speaking may be interrupted without that one's consent, unless the speaker is out of order.

E. Remarks should be brief, and no one should speak more than twice on the same question, except by permission.

IV. VOTING

A. Voting by the raising of the hand is to be

preferred, although this is at the discretion of the moderator or meeting.

B. In cases of special importance, voting by ballot or by standing may be resorted to.

C. The moderator calls first the affirmative and then the negative, announcing at the conclusion whether the motion is carried or lost.

D. All members are allowed to vote, except such as may be under discipline.

E. The moderator may give the deciding vote, but should rarely claim the privilege.

F. No motion, discussion, or other proceeding can be admitted while a vote is being taken.

V. QUESTIONS OF PRIVILEGE

A. While a motion is pending, it may be amended by another motion. An amendment should not essentially change the nature or design of the original motion. An amendment to an amendment may be made, but this should be the limit.

B. A substitute may be offered for any motion or amendment under debate, which may or may not change the meaning of the motion.

C. A question may be interrupted and deferred by a motion to lay it on the table. If this is for an indefinite time, it is regarded as a final dismissal of the question, though anyone may have the right, subsequently, to call it up again. A motion to lay it on the table for a specified time is not debatable.

D. A debate may be cut short by a vote to take "the previous question," that is, the question as originally announced without any additions or amendments that may have been made. If carried, the original question must be taken up and immediately disposed of without debate. A motion to take up the "previous question" is not debatable.

E. If, when a question is introduced, a member objects to its discussion as foreign, profitless, or contentious, the moderator should immediately put the question, "Shall this question be discussed?" If decided in the negative, the whole matter is at once dismissed. The motion as to whether the question shall be discussed is not debatable.

F. A question under discussion may be referred by vote to a committee.

G. A motion to reconsider a motion previously

passed must be made by one who voted for the motion when the previous action was taken. If the motion to reconsider prevails, the original motion is placed before the meeting as at first and may be discussed, rescinded, or reaffirmed.

H. A motion to adjourn is always in order (except when one is speaking) and takes precedence over all other motions and is not debatable, nor can it be amended, unless it be to fix a time and place for meeting again.

I. The moderator announces all votes and decides all questions of order in debate; but any member dissatisfied with a decision may appeal to the meeting. A vote is then taken upon the question, "Shall the decision of the moderator be sustained?" The decision of the meeting is final.

VI. COMMITTEES

A. Committees are nominated by the moderator or by the meeting itself; the nomination being confirmed by vote of the meeting.

B. The first one named in the appointment of a committee is considered the chairperson, though the committee has the right to elect its own chairperson when it has been called together.

C. Any subject in debate or matter of business may be referred to a committee, with or without instructions: the committee to report the result of its investigation to the meeting.

D. The report of a committee should be presented in writing.

E. The report of a committee may be received by a vote, which simply acknowledges the service of the committee and places its report before the meeting for action. Afterward, the report may be adopted as a whole or in its separate items.

F. When the recommendations of the committee are of minor consequence, or are likely to be generally acceptable, the report may be received and adopted by a single motion.

G. A report may be recommitted to the committee for a further investigation or a more acceptable presentation of the subject.

A DIRECTORY OF
BAPTIST ORGANIZATIONS

American Baptist Churches in the U.S.A.,
Office of General Secretary,
Board of International Ministries,
Board of National Ministries,
Board of Educational Ministries,
Valley Forge, PA 19482-0851

Baptist General Conference
1233 Central Street
Evanston, IL 60201

Conservative Baptist Association
Geneva Road, Box 66, Wheaton, IL 60187

General Association of Regular Baptists,
1800 Oakton Blvd., Des Plaines, IL 60018

National Baptist Convention of America,
Publishing Board, 523 Second Avenue North,
Nashville, TN 37201

National Baptist Convention U.S.A., Inc.,
Foreign Mission Board, 701 S. Nineteenth St.,
Philadelphia, PA 19146
Home Mission Board, 1323 E. Second St.,
Plainfield, NJ 07062
Sunday School Publishing Board,
330 Charlotte Ave., Nashville, TN 37201

North American Baptist General Conference,
7308 Madison St., Forest Park, IL 60130

Progressive National Baptist Convention, Inc.
1239 Vermont Ave., N.W., Washington, DC 20005

Southern Baptist Convention
Executive Offices, 460 James Robertson Pkwy.,
Nashville, TN 37219
Foreign Mission Board, 3806 Monument Ave.,
Richmond, VA 23230
Home Mission Board, 1350 Spring St., N.W.,
Atlanta, GA 30303
Sunday School Board, 127 Ninth Ave. N.,
Nashville, TN 37203

WILLS

Unless members of your family have a prior claim, the ideal use of a Christian's money is a gift for some religious use. Before making your will, consult a lawyer. All states have legal requirements concerning legacies to religious institutions. For instance, in Pennsylvania such a gift is void unless the will is made at least thirty days before the decease of the testator. Many an intended legacy in Pennsylvania has failed by reason of the disregard of this provision. Get the exact name of the church or board or society to which you are making your gift, and then use this language:

"I give, devise, and bequeath to The _____ _____ the sum of
$ _____ ."

After that, the less said the better, as the intent of a testator is often defeated by his attempt to explain it.

ANNUITIES

Any of our National Societies and Boards will accept your contribution of money as the consideration of an ANNUITY. The ANNUITY CONTRACT is the society's solemn covenant to pay you during your life a definite sum in yearly payments. Upon your decease, the annuity ceases and the principal fund is released for the general uses of the society. The annuity may also be made payable to some other person upon your decease. The amount of the annuity depends upon your age at the time the Annuity Contract is made. The rate is the same with all the National Societies. Consult your favorite society for full particulars.

ISBN 0-8170-0117-4